Human Body Adventures

Contents

Alison Blank

01567

Introduction

The body is an amazing machine. It is always busy breathing, pumping, mending and growing.

This **athlete's** body has to work very hard to run so fast.

Doctors and scientists have special machines that help them see inside the body.

In this book we won't use any special machines. Instead, we are going to imagine that we're very, very small. We are going on our own amazing journey inside the human body.

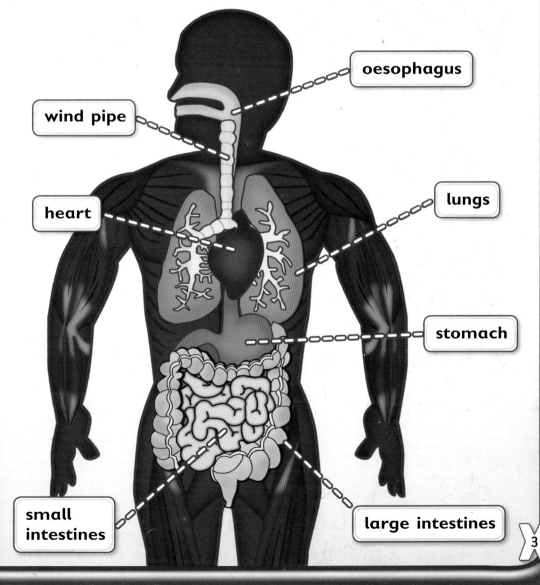

oesophagus

wind pipe

heart

lungs

stomach

small intestines

large intestines

The Great Blast

Location: the nose

Do you have your waterproofs on? We're entering the left nostril. It's dark and damp in here. All around us are huge strands of hair.

When the human breathes in, a strong wind blows past us. Seconds later, the human breathes out and wind blasts past us going the other way.

Humans need air to live. The hairs in the nose warm the air. They also help **filter** the air.

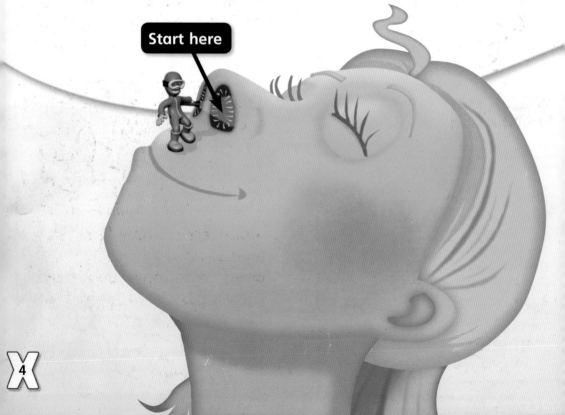

Start here

The further back we go, the darker and warmer it gets. We wade through **mucus**. It is so sticky that it's hard for us to take a step. Sometimes we find pieces of dirt, pieces of pollen or even a tiny bug stuck to a hair.

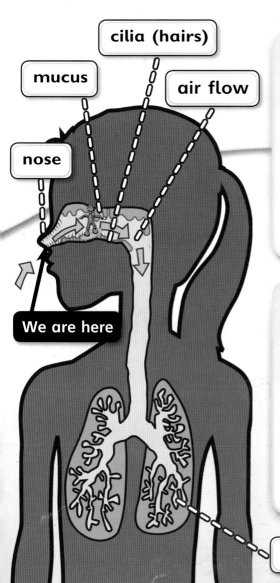

cilia (hairs)

mucus

air flow

nose

We are here

lungs

If you were an elephant, your nose would be more than 2 metres long.

If you were a whale, you would breathe from a blow-hole on top of your head.

Look! Under our feet, the mucus is moving!
Millions of waving hairs sweep it further and further
back. These hairs can **sense** if there is something that
shouldn't be here ... like us.

An extreme close-up picture of the inside
of a human nose. Can you see the hairs?

There are millions of **nerve cells** inside the human nose. When humans breathe in, they also breathe in **particles** from things that smell. These particles are so small you can't see them. But the nerve cells sense them and send messages to the brain. The brain tells the person that they can smell fresh-baked bread, stinky cheese, flowers or even old socks.

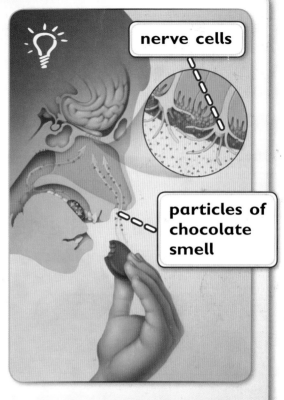

nerve cells

particles of chocolate smell

The human nose can recognise as many as 10 000 different smells.

Dogs have an amazing sense of smell. A dog's nose has 200 million smell cells. A human nose has 5 million smell cells.

Phew! We've made it past the mucus and hairs. But, yikes, our hike has made this human's nose tickle! Hold on …

We're flying out of the nose at 160 kilometres per hour!

Finally we land. Thank goodness for the soft tissue outside the nose. Shall we shake off the mucus and try somewhere else?

What happens when we sneeze?

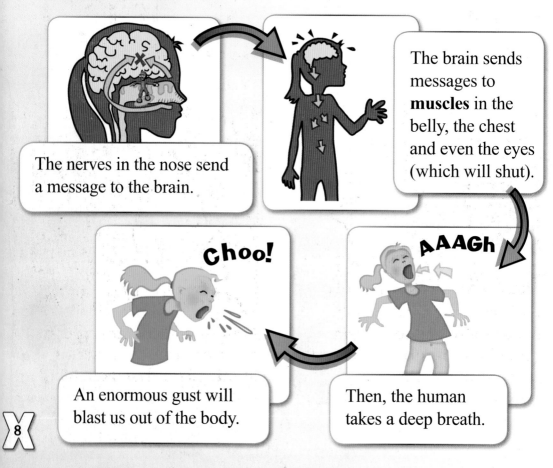

The nerves in the nose send a message to the brain.

The brain sends messages to **muscles** in the belly, the chest and even the eyes (which will shut).

Choo!

AAAGh

An enormous gust will blast us out of the body.

Then, the human takes a deep breath.

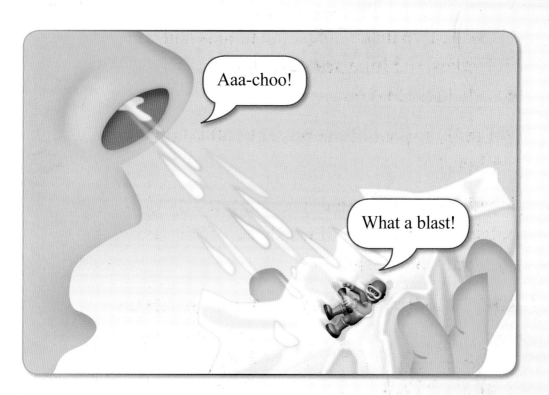

The air in a sneeze travels faster than a cheetah can run. Cheetahs are the fastest animals on earth!

Coughs and sneezes spread diseases. Trap your germs in a tissue or handkerchief!

The Great Splash

Location: the mouth

Welcome to the mouth, the beginning of the **digestive system**. We're standing on a huge pink hill. It's called the tongue.

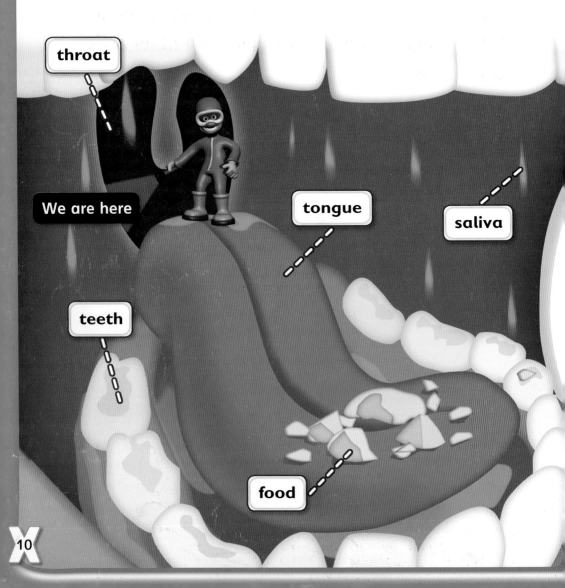

throat

We are here

tongue

saliva

teeth

food

The tongue moves as the human takes a bite of food. Watch out! Huge chunks of food are bouncing towards us. On either side, teeth the size of enormous rocks crush and grind the food. With each chew, the pieces of food get smaller.

Saliva drips down the sides of the mouth. Saliva contains digestive juices that start to break down the food. The tongue pushes us further and further back towards the throat.

Help! We're being swallowed!

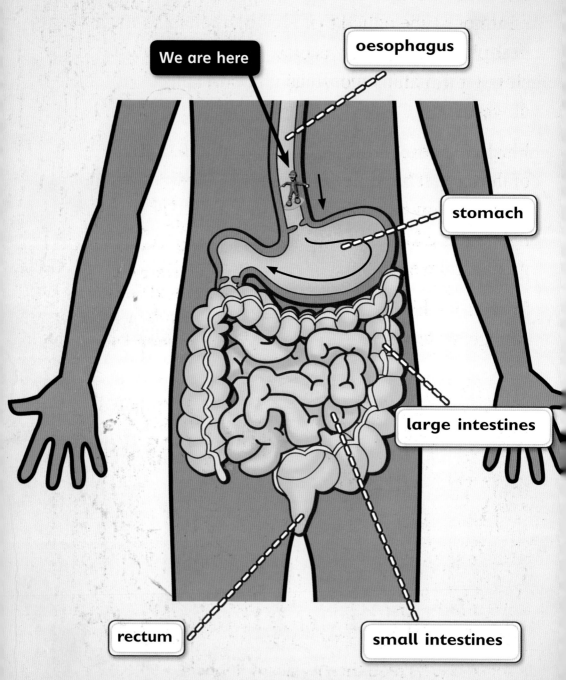

oesophagus

We are here

stomach

large intestines

rectum

small intestines

Now we're inside an enormous tube called the **oesophagus**. Strong muscles slowly push and squeeze us downward.

Finally we reach the bottom of the tube. It has only taken seconds. Now we wait until a tight muscle loosens. Suddenly it does and we are falling.

Splash! We hit the surface of a strange, watery sea.

If you were a cow, you would have four stomachs!

A snake kills its prey then swallows it whole. Its stomach expands to fit it all in!

We are in the stomach. Pieces of chewed up food bob all around us. Every now and then, the walls fold in on themselves.

Huge waves crash into us. We need to grab onto one of those pieces of half-chewed food to stay afloat!

The stomach is full of powerful juices. These juices break down and melt the food – this process is called digestion. The walls of the stomach are coated in slimey mucus. Without the mucus, the muscle would be digested. Thankfully, we have our protective suits on. Otherwise we'd be **digested**, too!

We only have 3–4 hours before this mush is going to leave the stomach. We need to get out of here!

If you were a crocodile, your digestive juices would be strong enough to melt steel!

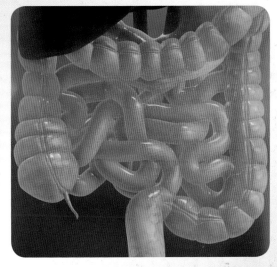

A human adult's intestines are 7.5 metres long.

1. The first way out is fast but messy. If the human was sick, we could go back up the way we came in. Thankfully, there are two other options.

I

EXIT From stomach to mouth

2

Through the small intestine

2. The second way out is to keep on moving with the rest of the melted food. From the stomach we would go to the small intestine. Food is absorbed through the walls of the small intestine. We would end up in the **bloodstream**.

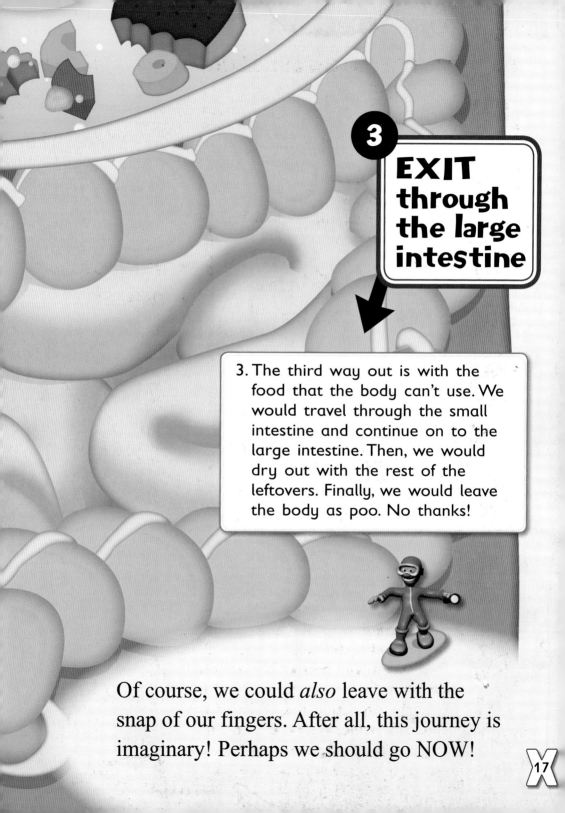

3

EXIT through the large intestine

3. The third way out is with the food that the body can't use. We would travel through the small intestine and continue on to the large intestine. Then, we would dry out with the rest of the leftovers. Finally, we would leave the body as poo. No thanks!

Of course, we could *also* leave with the snap of our fingers. After all, this journey is imaginary! Perhaps we should go NOW!

The Great Glide

Location: the skin

Skin is the body's largest **organ**. It is the perfect wrapping-paper and the perfect coat. Our skin stretches as we grow. It is waterproof and protects us. It keeps our insides in and most germs out. Imagine what a mess we would be if we didn't have skin to cover us!

This human body adventure starts in the epidermis. This is the top layer of skin. Below us are things like blood vessels, nerve endings, sweat **glands** and fat. These are all in the dermis, the inner layer of the skin.

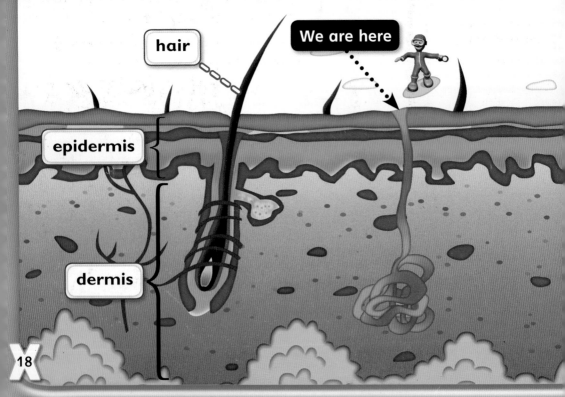

hair

We are here

epidermis

dermis

We step onto a skin cell. Every minute, new skin cells are being made. They push our old cells up towards the surface. Suddenly, we are moving!

Do you know why people have different skin colours? A chemical in the skin called melanin causes skin colour. The darker the skin colour, the more melanin there is.

blood vessel

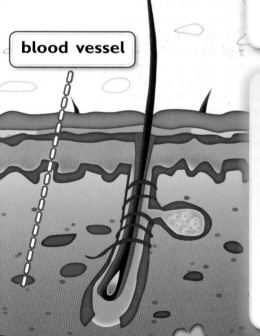

Freckles are also caused by melanin.

We pop off the skin like a roof tile in the wind. In just one minute, 30 000–40 000 other skin cells pop off too.

We gently land on a carpet. We can see that we are not alone. All around us are other dead skin cells. Wow! We have become the dust that gathers on the floor.

This is dust seen through a microscope. Dust is made up of many different tiny things, including old skin cells.

If you were a snake, you would shed your whole skin in one go up to 8 times a year.

The human body is an amazing place.
Hope you've enjoyed the ride!

Glossary

athlete	a person who is good at sport
bloodstream	the blood flowing through your body
cells	tiny parts that all living things are made of
digest	when your stomach breaks down food so your body can use it
filter	to stop dirt passing through something
glands	a part of the body that produces chemicals for the body to use
intestine	a long tube in the body which helps to break down food
lungs	you use your lungs for breathing
mucus	a thick slippery liquid made by the body
muscle	a strong part of your body that you use to make your body move
nerve	a part of your body that carries messages to and from your brain
oesophagus	the tube through which food passes from the mouth to the stomach
organ	part of the body with a particular job
particle	a very small piece of something
saliva	a clear watery liquid in the mouth
sense	to be aware of something

Index